FINAL
JUDGEMENTS

Joan Fuster (1922-1992) was a highly influential poet, critic and thinker who wrote in both Catalan and Spanish. Born in Sueca, a village near Valencia, he grew up in a middle-class Catholic family and graduated with a law degree from the Universitat de València in 1947. Renowned for his irony, and his concise, incisive style of writing, Fuster is best known as an essayist and left-wing thinker who championed Catalan language and culture in Francoist Spain. Among his most celebrated books are *Nosaltres, els valencians* (1962), *Diccionari per a ociosos* (1964), and *Final Judgements* (1960).

Mary Ann Newman (1951) is a translator from Catalan and Spanish into English. A graduate in Hispanic literatures of New York University, she has become one of the foremost voices on Catalan culture in the English-speaking world. She has translated fiction by Quim Monzó and Josep Maria de Sagarra, essay by Xavier Rubert de Ventós, and poetry by Josep Carner. Newman was awarded the Creu de Sant Jordi in 1998, the J.B. Cendrós International Award from Òmnium Cultural and the North American Catalan Society Award for Scholarship in 2016, and the Ramon Llull International Award in 2022.

This translation has been published in Great Britain
by Fum d'Estampa Press Limited 2022
002

Original Catalan title: Consells, proverbis i insolències, 1968
All rights reserved

The moral rights of the author and translator have been asserted
Set in Adobe Garamond Pro

Printed and bound by Great Britain by CMP UK Ltd.
A CIP catalogue record for this book is available from the British Library

ISBN: 978-1-913744-35-9

Published in collaboration with the Acadèmia Valenciana de la Llengua

Escriptor
de l'Any 2022

FUM D'ESTAMPA PRESS

FINAL JUDGEMENTS

JOAN FUSTER

Translated by

MARY ANN NEWMAN

Prologue by
Adam Gopnik

CONTENTS

PROLOGUE

Forward!

When a new poet enters our vision—or swims into our ken, as Keats would have it—the world seems to expand, and horizontal possibilities of allusion begin to leap freely in our minds. We read the cosmic-confessional poetry of Robert Lowell or Sylvia Plath, and we begin to forge new connections in our own heads between what happened in history and what happened to us. When a new aphorist appears, or is introduced to us, on the other hand, the world seems instead to contract—not in a limiting or narrowing sense, but more as in the closing iris of a Chaplin film: a narrative of emotion and truth collapses into a single radiant point.

Having never heard of the Valencian aphorist Joan Fuster before I read the book you hold, his work has had the force on me of that kind: like points of light in the night sky, he glitters rather than connects. We emerge from reading him with a handful of stars in our hands.

His aphorisms can be composed into constellations by our own efforts, made into a coherent 'ideology'—but they shine brightest on their own. As always with aphorisms, the only thing to do is quote, display them, however nugatory that act may seem in prefacing the whole. But with Fuster the urge is irresistible.

Fuster is a specially varied aphorist. His basic tone is that of a wise man dispensing a lifetime's disabused wisdom: "Some of our defects are so well-rooted, and feel so much a part of us, that we don't dare correct them for fear they might be virtues. And, in the end, who knows if this is not what virtues are?" Often, he is worldly, and persuasive in his worldliness: "We write with our enemies in mind. Either to convince them or to corrupt them." He can be as realistic and disabused as Rochefoucauld: "Clarity is born of argument," they say. And experience shows that, in effect, people tend to hold on to the same convictions they had before they argued, but now with more clarity."

But he can also be profound: "There is death. Hence there will

9

always be God. There is life. Hence there will always be gods." He can be at once appreciative and erudite, not always a natural marriage particularly about music, as in his insistence that Mozart is above all an Italian composer. And, the note that is his special contribution to the aphoristic tradition—set off in this book by the beautiful idiomatic translations of Mary Ann Newman—he has a kind of instinctive playful gift for the crazy, off-beam generalization that somehow seems to settle just right, a little like the kind of thing we find in Emily Dickinson's letters or Kafka's notebooks: "In Rodin's nudes you can tell that the clothes the figures have just taken off are the rough industrial garments of the 19th century. On the sculptures' surfaces there is something akin to the outline of a cheap undershirt." Or simply (and my favorite): "In truth, if you give it enough thought, it turns out that the important poets have always confined themselves to writing about the moon."

Though one would search vainly for a polemical 'ideology' in Fuster, one can make those constellations out of his points, and a particular politics does breathe through the pages. They are very much the politics of a conservative Catholic-trained (if not Catholic-believing) intellectual of the mid-twentieth century, which are not the same as those of a reactionary ideologue. In English, Chesterton, a little earlier, and Larkin, around the same time, are of the same sort. (And he very much reminds this reader of the slightly older and mostly unknown British aphorist Geoffrey Madan, whose notebooks have some of the same dry, acerbic distance.). Fuster, raised a "Carlist", and a Catalan nationalist throughout his life, belongs in the conservative vein of those who value the local and the near at hand more than the abstract and far-away, but he is a cosmopolitan in tastes, and never surrenders to a mangy nationalism. He reminds us, as gay wits so often do—Wilde comes to mind often with Fuster—that it is possible to be both 'radical' in one's estimation of humanity and immensely social in one's acceptance of it.

He offers for our time of the best conservative case—reminding us ruefully that so much of what we do in life, particularly in 'improving' it, is affectation and mannerism more than genuine compassion or reform. We are more selfish creatures than we like to pretend, and the pretense is both the subject of satire and the means to a saner acceptance of our humanity. His point, like that of every maxim writer, is that we are basically kidding ourselves all the time in everything we do. Sincerity is a show; passion is self-seeking; "Every name is a pseudonym; every face, a mask; every gesture, an affectation; every word, an equivocation. And in these conditions, man is a social animal!"

You couldn't be both more dismissive—yet at the end more accepting—than that. Aphoristic wit is conservative since it relies on the epigrammatic enclosure of writer and reader; it doesn't have to explain itself, since we already have a certain guilty complicity with its points, even if we would be ashamed to admit it too publicly. Though it is cloaked in elegance, Fuster's 'point' is most often simply, Come off it! But then he adds, Come on: Embrace yourself as you actually are! It's a lovely, and deeply humanist, double message to receive.

Adam Gopnik

PREFACE

Personally, aphorisms have attracted me since childhood. And, without a doubt, the origin of my inclination wouldn't be hard for me to identify. Every year, my household would acquire a bloc-calendar of *The Messenger of the Sacred Heart of Jesus*, and, day after day, I was in the habit of reading the brief lesson of morality or dogma parceled out on each page, between the saints' days and the phases of the moon and the hour of the sunrise, by the priests of the Company of Jesus. I no longer remember what those papers—"scraps of paper, as I have called them elsewhere"—said. I suppose they recommended chastity, love of God, patience, humility, discretion. What else could *The Messenger of the Sacred Heart of Jesus* recommend? And it isn't that I found all of that interesting, not by a long shot. But, in those days, I didn't have anything else at hand to read, beyond my schoolbooks and the occasional comic. Thirty-five or forty years ago, that daily wall calendar of clerical manufacture—my parents were rather devout—served its audience a daily ration of "reflections", two or three lines beneath the number of the date and the indication of the month and the day of the week. On the back of the leaf were historical anecdotes, run-of-the-mill jokes about mayseeds, recipes, riddles, passages from the Gospels, and "scientific curiosities". It may have been an apostolic device current at the time. The only thing I read were the doses of "doctrine" that appeared on the front. My childhood was bedazzled by them. For me, the trivialities and fervid exhortations of *The Messenger*, condensed and incisive, amounted to a veritable seduction. The more I think about it, the clearer it seems to me that this is the distant and ludicrous source of my recurrent delight in the aphorism.

Or perhaps not so ludicrous after all. In the final analysis, what I envied or admired about the anonymous Jesuit author of the calendar was the guarantee that it would be read every day by someone in the many, infinite houses like my own. A reading that was regular and anticipated, but lasted only a few seconds. I suspect that this was my first literary aspiration, to write "sayings" for calendars. And I must not entirely have rid myself of it. In fact, my aphorisms are just this, "thoughts" destined for loose pages, domestic, insignificant, and steadfastly guaranteed to be consumed. In a word: this is all they pretend to be. Without realizing it, this is the use I have assigned them. But I don't want to kid myself. This is, in fact, just a gratuitous, strictly pointless conjecture. I have never really intended to write "for wall calendars". Circumstances and profession have led me to other, more rarefied, or at least unrelated, publishing platforms. As the "topic" of my speculations was, or became, for this very reason, inviable for a calendar and by the same token for the attention of an average, ordinary household. This was a fate I couldn't escape—not then, not now. But I retain a great affection for the routine of aphorisms. At least from season to season. And I can't quite let it go. It is not lost on me that books like the one I now offer to the reader will never be "digestible" in the way a novel, an epic poem, an erudite monograph or a treatise on theology are. A too-thick package of aphorisms does not lend itself to continuous reading. It gets tiresome. Tiresome, probably, owing to its very intellectual dispersion, syncopated overture, and the requisite complement of meditation... I miss the calendar. And, when all is said and done, this accretion of counsels, proverbs, and impertinent remarks doesn't go much farther.

J. F.
Sueca, December 17, 1967

FINAL
JUDGEMENTS

PREJUDICES

It is written: "Judge not, that you may not be judged" (or perhaps it was: "Judge not and you will not be judged," I don't recall). Fine. Still and all, and be that as it may, it seems we will be—and already are—inexorably subject to judgement. Why, then, deprive ourselves of the pleasure of judging others?

You all know the famed Greek aphorism: "Joan Fuster is the measure of all things."

And yet I endorse methodical mistrust.

KNOWLEDGE OF CAUSES

Paul Valéry said, almost apologetically, "I do not say that I am right, I say this is the way I am." But maybe he should simply have said—maybe we should all simply say—"I am right *because* this is the way I am."

Everything we do is irreparable.

The cause of our joys is usually ridiculously banal. And, in the cold light of day, this is a shame.

Always defend your right to change your mind. It is the first thing your enemies will deny you.

We also tire of despair.

We will never begin to know someone until we see them *beside* themselves.

There are those who assert—and they surely have their reasons—that man is a contingent being. As for me, all I can say is, if I did not exist, I would have to be invented.

There is no point in poking fun at idiosyncrasies. We will never understand what it is to be Persian.

Even more to the point, how can anyone be different from me? How can someone be *another*—be *the* other?

If common sense—what we are given to calling common sense—were truly *common*, we would go insane.

In essence, a euphemism is already a lie.

Shakespeare didn't have to make any particular effort to be Shakespeare, nor Goethe to be Goethe, nor Dante to be Dante. And this is a bit discouraging.

Many wounds of love are nothing more than wounds to our self-esteem.

When has a confidence, a personal confession to a friend, not been born of vanity? Even if the most despicable thing is being confessed.

You are always stupid with regard to someone.

I'm not sure whether the obsession with death, so typical in adolescence, should be listed under the heading of depravity or petulance.

The word was not bestowed on man to reveal or hide his thoughts, but to justify them.

Getting old is resigning yourself to getting old. There is no other explanation.

Still, it is advisable to age at the same rate as your body.

Audaces fortuna iuvat. If the gods favor the bold, it is just for a laugh.

To be friends with a very egotistical person—more egotistical than you yourself—makes things very simple. It allows you to fake friendship without remorse.

Gratitude is paralyzing.

"Our desire has no cure," says Saint Theresa of Avila somewhere. This is, in effect, a great truth, at least in the literal sense.
And, if we accept this premise—major or minor—any syllogism derived from it can only have one conclusion: "Life is *pointless.*"

Love. Despite it all, in the words of Dante: "*Io son più ch'io…*"

Thought is affirmed—and reaffirmed—through opposition. Give me a good contrarian, and I will invent the most exalted theories.

Much as poor Lear wondered: "Who is it that can tell me who I am?"

It may seem illogical, but the first condition for being a cynic is that others not be.

There is a "fear of knowing" which is the fear of *becoming* or becoming *converted* to what we have come to know.

"…Human, all too human…" Nothing is *too* human.

The only way to *have* anything—liberty or power, happiness or objects, love—is to seize it from another.

"Clarity is born of argument," they say. And experience shows that, in effect, people tend to hold on to the same convictions they had before they argued, but now with more clarity.

Part of being polite is knowing when to be rude.

We are unrepeatable.

Blessed are those who have had a teacher—a *maître à penser*, as it were—for they will be able to renounce him.

We must take things as they are—and hence see death, suffering and injustice as the extortion of the demigods.

Strictly speaking, to appear to give in may be an excellent tactic for either a politician or a lover.

We almost always envy the defects of our enemies and, of course, *sub specie boni*. Deep down, what we despise, and what annoys us about them, are their virtues.

As for me, alcohol makes me more understanding.

Balzac vs. Maragall: I do not understand that character in Balzac who aspired to "live to excess". Lord, I who only desire to suspend each moment to live the eternal, etc., etc.

We may never be as sincere as we are when we are pretending to be sincere.

A surrealist once declared that "Elephants are contagious." And he may be right. You never know.

For something to move us, it has to be a little bit corny.

Since man is man, he has done nothing more than correct creation, amending the work of God—everything that God made and that, according to Genesis, he saw as good…

When man reaches the conclusion that a problem is insoluble, he becomes a slave to it. What results from this is a *destiny* that can indeed be called tragic and which, in point of fact, is the destiny of his most ancient tragedies.

Formulate an error as an axiom, and you will end up perceiving it as a truth.

Only death is perfect—and, even then, not always.

All my ideas are provisional. (But, for the record, it's not something I'm proud of.)

If you give it a little thought, you will realize that it is not being contradicted that annoys you, but rather to be shown that you are contradicting yourself.

The ability to forget is, beyond any doubt, a clear symptom of physical and moral health.

The world would be a great deal more intolerable if one—I, you, he—did not believe that one's own life was exceptional.

Furtive love affairs have in their favor that they come to seem charming.

—"*Je ne méprise presque rien…*" And, neither do I, if you please.

If it ever seems you are in agreement with another, make no mistake about it: There has been a misunderstanding.

Women are pure physiology. Men, too, but they try to hide it.

I imagine there must be some difference or another between being an atheist with regard to Jehovah and being an atheist with regard to any other divinity (or all of Olympus).

What's more, I think we must not confuse two such distinct things as atheism and theophobia. More than one *soi-disant* atheist is nothing but a simple, more or less rabid, theophobe.

All men are mortal, and I more than any other.

An Author's Modesty. Aphorisms—mine or anyone else's—are always false, intrinsically false. And this one, too.

It is dangerous to earn the enmity of a stupid man, because stupid men tend to be more treacherous than evil ones. Even worse, it is morally uncomfortable. You always feel a bit foolish with a stupid person as an enemy.

We can only be refuted by someone who thinks like us.

Any ambition, no matter how dubious, will inspire respect if taken to a violent extreme.

"What's going on?"
"Time."
And, in effect, *what goes on* is time.

Every name is a pseudonym; every face, a mask; every gesture, an affectation; every word, an equivocation. And in these conditions, man is a social animal! Yes, gentlemen: *zoon politikon.*

"*Ego dixi: Dii estis*" (Ps., LXXXII, 6), "I said, 'You are gods.'" And we refuse to believe it!

The most useful lessons are the ones we decide not to heed, precisely because we do not heed them.

If an adult man is nostalgic for his childhood, he either doesn't remember it, or he misremembers it.

It bears noting that beneath the innocence of an Abel there often lies an outrageous and blatant provocation. Or to put it another way, in most cases, such innocence is, *per se*, a provocation.

All metaphysics are "metaphysics of consolation," including that of Camus himself, to the extent that it is a metaphysics.

This is why I think that, *in the eye of the consumer*, there is no particularly essential difference between philosophy and cognac or morphine.

There are those who are lawyers, or teachers, or bishops, or poets, or farmers. My profession, in contrast, is to be Joan Fuster.

In many things, but particularly in love, experience tends to be a defect. That's why one remembers one's first love to be the best—it *is* the best.

Everything we say—and write!—is a commonplace. Otherwise we would not understand one another.

Truth at School. "*Adaequatio intellectus et rei.*" The intellect must be adequate to the thing. Right. But what does *adaequatio* mean? And what does *intellectus* mean? And what, indeed, does *et* mean?

There are not different ways of believing.

No one offends us so much as someone who refuses to be our enemy, precisely when we want them to be our enemy.

Life is monotonous, beyond any doubt, and how, but we usually don't realize that we ourselves are even more monotonous.

Topic for Meditation. *In this precise moment,* millions and millions of people are fornicating in thought, word, or deed. The remaining millions are awaiting their turn. (The *moment* in question is always any moment.)

The vanity of others *only* seems unbearable to us precisely because it feels like a usurpation.

Look closely: God's will is always done—for someone else.

"*Duo si idem dicunt, non est idem.*" If two people say the same thing, it is not the same. But that's not all. The same thing, said by the same person at different times, is no longer the same.

We know we must die, but our instinct for preservation advises us to ignore it.

A system of thought, I mean one without internal contradictions, will always have the disadvantage of not being able to resolve its contradiction with life.

There is one danger: that of coming to resemble oneself too much.

But is it also quite difficult to imitate oneself.

Le moi haïssable. I am not a prudent man: I haven't sunk so low. I am simply a coward, which is an entirely different—and to a certain extent, quite the opposite—thing.

From time to time we feel the need to come up with a straw man just for the pleasure of refuting him. If we didn't, we might come to lose faith in our own convictions.

That man has managed throughout the centuries to invent so many and so varied metaphysics is something that ought not to surprise us. In the end, we are talking about simple excrescences of the imagination. What seems more surprising, though, and perhaps even alarming, is that man should have the need, or *still* has the need, to continue inventing them.

Oh, if one's sex could think! (Forgive me, but the suggestion comes via Pascal: "Imagine a body full of thinking members.")

There is death. Hence there will always be God. There is life. Hence there will always be gods.

Rarely can a truth be formulated—a certain kind of truth, in any case—without seeming insolent.

Perhaps this is why, on occasion, there are those who can appear to be speaking truths by affecting insolence.

Possessives. Behold a truly disturbing grammatical form.

We bestow importance, a great deal of importance, upon certain things *in order to* find a way to believe that in this arid, desolate life there are indeed important things.

All theories, taken to their ultimate consequences, turn out to be absurd. What this means is that *they were already absurd* from the start, at least in part. And clearly this conclusion must lead us to adopt a moderate skepticism. To adopt it. Not to profess it, which would not be worth the trouble.

Youth is always stupid, even when the young person in question is named Rimbaud—who was, in effect, stupid, and also a genius (the conditions are not incompatible).

Sociology of Fashion. It's all about business. The supposed sexual implications are merely an excuse.

Imagine a smiling Stoic. That would be the perfect man.

For the eye to observe itself, it requires the mediation of a mirror. Consciousness also requires a mirror. We only see—or know—ourselves through another.

"To live is not yet to have died." "For man, to live is to await death"; etc.

A love without disappointments would not be love. It would be—how can I put it?—marmalade or a Bach fugue.

Love, again. "*S'io m'intuassi come tu t'immii…*" But this is impossible! To start with, because (though I can't quite get the translation right) no *t'emmeves*—you do not belong *to me*—nor *t'immies*—nor do you belong *in me*. I only think you do.

People like myself, for example, who are practically skeptics, are doomed to find whatever others do to be good, while bearing with the fact that there is always someone who will find fault with everything we do.

Truths must be exaggerated in order to seem credible.

Women, like men of letters, are essentially anachronistic creatures.

It makes me very sad to be listening to an intelligent person speak and not find anything they say interesting.

Who could bear the notion of a duplicate of himself?

To reflect upon something—it seems the word itself states it—is tantamount to casting a reflection.
Or to reflecting oneself?

All philosophies are barely veiled forms—camouflages, we might say—of solipsism.

We aspire to certainty in all things (to moral certainty, at least). And I don't know why. In truth, it doesn't matter.

Not only a person's richness of thought, but also the complexity of their sentimental nuances, depends on their command of vocabulary and syntax. We think and we feel to the extent that our language allows.

A person who loves us is a permanent danger.

The only pleasures that don't disappoint are the unforeseen ones.

Adam—The abominable snowman. I mean, the abominable man of Eden.

I often think of saying what that character in the novel said: "Prove that I'm telling the truth!" Not as a challenge, though, but as a plea.

The more I think about it, the more I believe that to be me is a kind of neurosis—and a rather disconcerting one, at that.

ETHICS FOR A STRANGER

Repeat after me: "*Nihil humani…*" *Nothing human is alien…* Not even stupidity.

In everything we do—even in things that are not right—our only redemption lies in utter obstinacy.

Accept yourself as you are. But find a way, immediately, to convert this acceptance into remorse.

The ideas you have; the ideas that have you. The latter—though you don't know it—are the ones you act upon.

We ought to feel a bit—even if just a little bit—responsible for the faces of our children and for the fanaticism of our comrades-in-arms: in some way we, too, are to blame.

Don't get irritated. It's bad for your health.

A moralist is a man with a disappointing experience of other men.

The innocent doesn't know he's innocent—and that's why he is.

Psychology of the confessional. Every first sin responds, like Eve's, to the same motivation: curiosity. The second sin—a repetition of the first—is committed out of pride. From then on, it's just a question of habit.

Do you suffer? Well, resign yourself to it. No one was born unpunished. Seneca said so.

There are those who deserve admiration, or disdain, or indifference. But there are also those who deserve nothing but resentment.

Do they accuse you? Pay them no mind. It can only be in the name of norms or myths that, tacitly or expressly, you have already disavowed.

Pride always conceals one kind of impotence or another: it is the great deceit of the weak. When they speak, for example, of "aristocratic pride", we must understand that the nobles in question are no longer sure of their caste superiority. A genuine aristocrat is a despot, or a beast, but he is not self-important.

To what extent do *others* have a right to my sincerity?

Against good and against evil—against the pretensions of one or the other—there is only one defense: irony.

To live is to betray.

Behold the most delightful face, the most enchanting smile. Good. Beneath it lies a gloomy, expressionless skull. We all know this. But I find thinking of it to be a veritable sin of obscenity.

And what's more, all skulls—like all sexes—are the same, more or less.

Don't ask for your best friend's understanding. At most he will feel sorry for you, just like everyone else.

If you really think about it, you will find that no one *deserves* your envy.

There is a basic error at the core of all infatuation. For no good reason, we thought the person we loved *was someone else.*

It's good to believe we are loved by others. It helps us love them back.

I'm sorry, but I've never admired a single man of action.

If by chance you are a virtuous person—whatever kind of virtue you may profess—it is best you keep it under your hat. This way you will avoid two considerable irritations: being admired and being despised.

You have not chosen your life, and yet you are responsible for it. Though they dare not admit it, this is the fundamental paradox that ethics can never quite resolve.

Turn every misfortune that befalls you into an accusation of another. This will make it bearable.

Obedience is safe.

Enough *homages*, already! Hypocrisy is a *duty* that virtue imposes on vice.

And rarely do we consider the tragedy—or at least the drama—of one who is a hypocrite *malgré lui*.

A Lenten Reflection. The flesh is sad, alas! That may well be, but try telling it so.

Beware! Never reveal what you think you are. It is dangerous. Because others can compare it with what you really are, and the comparison will unvaryingly be unfavorable.

Our neighbors' flaws have at least one advantage. They give us the opportunity to feel puritanical, if only for a moment.

If you think—about yourself, about the world, about anything—you will feel different from others. Reflection isolates.

Heterodoxy is always solitude.
Or vice versa: Solitude is always heterodoxy.

The disjunction may well lie between solitude and solidarity.

We often forget it, but it is not at all clear that victims of injustice are necessarily just themselves. Sometimes, for love of justice, you end up pitting one criminal against another.

"You must experience everything," they advise me. I reject uncomfortable experiences and idiotic experiences. This disqualifies me and rules me out for many things, but I couldn't care less.

Don't desert: Rebel. If you can, that is.

Marriage is the only legal and honorable form of complicity that our society recognizes.

The origin of the gods is not just fear, as Eustace said. It is also an instinct for rebellion. In symmetry with the spontaneous need to pray is the spontaneous need to blaspheme.

Autognosis. Know thyself. This way you will become accustomed to treating yourself—*in mente*, of course—with a certain disdain.

Sometimes we feel the need to possess something, just to be able to lose it.

Don't try to improvise your life. If you do, you run the risk of finding that "inspiration" fails you just when the risk is greatest.

How discouraging. We all have the same flaws!

Luck is a thing—an opportunity?—which only *others* enjoy. (This principle applies to everyone.)

"Do you change? Then you are truth." To be true to yourself does not necessarily imply being faithful to *your* things: to *your* ideas, to *your* ethics, to *your* idea of yourself which you yourself have invented...

We mustn't kid ourselves: Honor is a most costly luxury.

Pretend that you are interested in the intimate trivialities your neighbor recounts. Maybe this way you will get him to pretend for you when you tell him yours. In the end you will find that you have become friends, and when all is said and done this is the essence of friendship.

More than an aberration, I think avarice is ill-advised.

Try not to feel indignant with someone because they are egotistical, evil, or stupid. You are just like them. And so am I.

It is preferable to speak, to speak clearly, and to say everything you mean. Words, or words half-said, that remain inside your body will rot there.

On a different note, the real problem is: When do we have the *right* to be silent?

There are those who accept the misfortunes that befall them, as if they had chosen them freely. This kind of spiritual masochism tends to be called by extremely respectable names.

Good faith, good faith... You know, all fanatics are people of good faith.

Of all the things one might find repugnant about prostitution, one is essential: It constitutes a bitterly flagrant form of simony.

"*Killing time...*" This expression is nothing less than a strategy: It posits time as our enemy. And that may be the only path to salvation.

Sometimes compassion leads to perversion.

Precisely because the world is unjust, or imperfect—however you want to put it—man needs hope to live. In truth, hope is nothing but a way of deceiving the body. But it can either console or lead to revolt—which is another form of consolation.

There is nothing healthier morally than having a clear notion of the exact proportion of being right that we can never wrest from our enemies.

Not everyone is capable of boredom. Tedium, in effect, requires a refined technique and a rather peculiar personal predisposition. In essence, you have to have a lot of imagination, use it all up, and then feel nostalgia for it.

Narcissus was an idler. When you have nothing to do, you tend to observe yourself and, by dint of self-contemplation, you end up finding yourself admirable, handsome, and even quite dignified. The rest of the myth is similarly inevitable.

Love your enemy. Fine. But it would be good to be able to love him without ceasing to consider him an enemy.

The only thing we are not is what we make an effort not to be.

Often we seek success, any old kind of success, even the most absurd, because we haven't managed to be happy.

There is no true love without a hint of depravity in the most tender moments.

Clara cum laude notitia: This is human glory, according to St. Thomas of Aquinas. It is decidedly not worth obsessing over.

Often people beg off doing something by alleging disdain or modesty. Don't let yourself be taken in! Underneath the refusals, often there is nothing more than pure and simple impotence.

Hypothetically, even the purest and most unselfish action can be ascribed to one heinous motivation or another. And, in most cases, such motivation is indeed there.

Have no hope or fear, and you will be perfect.

Dialectical Precept. When you argue and are in the right, you shout. As do, ordinarily, those not in the right. No one wants to lose their position out of respect for good manners.

Proper charity begins at home. Proper hatred, too.

It would be unjust to reproach Galileo for having retracted his scientific affirmations in order to save his life. Ultimately, a truth—if it is indeed a truth—will continue to be true whether a man dies for it or not. From an intellectual point of view martyrdom is never an argument. Even more, for Galileo, his own life had to be worth *more* than any truth.

Nowadays, adultery is just cheesy.

Who can truly take back something they have said? When it suits us, we revoke our words, but it is only in appearance.

The Art of Avoiding Inconsequentiality. Instead of adopting some principles and subjecting our conduct to them, it is preferable to deduce the principle from the conduct we follow. Perhaps, in doing this, our principles will never be particularly exalted, but this, too, is an advantage.

One only feels truly alone when one has nothing to think about—or when one is afraid to think about anything.

To speak ill of others is not as shameful a flaw as they say. While you are doing it, in effect, you do not fall into the temptation of speaking ill of yourself, which would be a greater flaw.

It is the duty of the young systematically to frighten the old, if only to keep them from totally falling asleep.

Reject on principle anything that is defined as ineffable, mysterious, or simply esoteric. All cows are black in the dark.

Think of *something else*, and you will find peace.

In general, it is not our own prejudices that oblige us to behave in one way or another. What obliges us, in point of fact, are the prejudices of others.

Some of our defects are so deep-seated, and feel so much a part of us, that we don't dare correct them for fear they might be virtues. And, in the end, who knows if this is not what virtues are.

Only with death will you be free of yourself. Resign yourself, then, to *never* being free.

What truly imbues us with melancholy is not so much yearning for the past as giving up on the future—and in practice it is not at all easy to distinguish one from the other.

Never advise someone not to do something that you yourself have not done. Nor should you advise someone to do something you yourself have done. Insofar as you can, never give advice.

Two brothers are never so united—they never feel quite so *brotherly*—as when they band together against their father.

There are moments in which one feels inferior to oneself. What a subtle, twisted form of vanity.

We do many things in order to talk about them. Robinson Crusoe was virtuous, less for lack of opportunity than for lack of interlocutors with whom to make small talk or share confidences.

"*Nihil humani...*", yet again. Respectable people are, at heart, those who find that there are certain things—human things—that are alien to them.

Assassins are also instruments of the designs and forces of Nature.

Believe me, young man: Ignore your own counsel! At your age one spends all his time deceiving himself.

Measure each man by his most despicable act, but treat him with the consideration due his most noble deed. And, for the record, this is not duplicity, but realism and sense of humor.

CLOV—*Tu crois à la vie future?*
HAMM—*La mienne l'a toujours eté.*
(S. Beckett, *Fin de partie.*)

It's always useful to have one obsession or another. It serves as a distraction.

Life can deny you everything, but it will always reserve you one opportunity: that of desperately making fun of others, and being right about it.

As we read in the Bible, "Faithful are the blows of a friend; dangerous, the kisses of an enemy." But we all—every one of us—hate to be struck, and are moved by kisses. And, when you come right down to it, being struck is not the most plausible sign of friendship.

In this world, it would seem that everyone is honorable until they are not.

If there is sin, everything is sin.
(Even Theology—above all, Theology!—takes the Lord's name in vain.)

Only by instinct do we act with reason. Most reflexive, lucid decisions made conscientiously turn out to be mad or clumsy.

"And you, who have nothing and expect nothing, why are you living?"
"So as not to die."

We must know how to reach *everything* in good time: love, success, misfortune, death. An insignificant acceleration or delay can frustrate your full enjoyment of the event.

Even the most sensual pleasures can be enjoyed in an intelligent way.

Every setback is a warning. You have no right to *expect* what you are hoping for.

To get oneself killed—for whatever reason: a crime, an ideal, a passion—is still a form of suicide. There's no denying it.

While We're On the Topic... *Sacra sacre tractanda.* To wit, in silence.

Happiness, as the Stoics asserted, consists in not desiring. In not feeling any desire, I would further specify. The absence of appetite is a state of perfection. Perhaps the only one.

To gamble is always a waste—of time, if nothing more.

For better or worse—usually for the better—none of our acts is anything more than a crude parody of our intention.

Paternity induces inanity.

Geese have always had beaks. Epochs usually described as profoundly depraved only surpass other periods in one form of depravation: the lack of shame.

The only truly useful form of fear I know of is a sense of responsibility.

A word to the wise: Truth and justice do not always coincide.

Only people lacking in sensuality can be fully and effortlessly materialistic.

I persist in believing that all dilemmas are false. They are traps to oblige you to do or to accept something you find repugnant.

Pain is only indignant and repulsive when it seems to have no purpose. Still, the person who is in pain will always consider it purposeless.

WORKS AND DAYS

Writing—making literature—is all those things you say it is, and a form of vengeance, to boot.

One of the dangers an artist is exposed to is that of becoming a *precursor*. This is the equivalent of being an born epigone before your time.

Don't kid yourselves, friends who attend concerts. Music—all music, from Palestrina or Bach to Armstrong or Stravinsky—is meant to be danced or sung.

Piero della Francesca would have been a perfect genius as a painter if only he had known how to paint a good smile.

Claudel is Victor Hugo, but worse, and orthodox.

Every word is already, *per se*, a periphrasis.

Some of Josep Carner's ironies make me think that he, the poet, has the elegant ennui of someone "who has read it all" and even so finds it entertaining—but *only* entertaining—to write more himself.

I have never met an enthusiastic reader of Nietzsche—and they do exist!—who is not, as a person, a ridiculous sort of fellow.

The worst thing about plagiarism is not that it is theft, but rather that it is redundant.

It must be admitted: "To admire"—that is, to feel admiration for someone or something—is a very laborious undertaking and, in the long run, a bore.

The opposite of a good painter (or a bad painter) is not a bad painter (or a good painter), but Picasso.

Literature is a petit bourgeois prejudice.
(Josep Maria Castellet, to whom I say this, responds that this itself is a petit bourgeois idea. Perhaps it is, and if so, all the more to my favor.)

In art, as in any other activity, it is advisable to imitate for as long as possible. Only when there is no other choice does it become tolerable to be original.

The absurd, an ancient, uncatalogued muse…

The most contemptible and repulsive literary genres can be practiced with genius. In point of fact, for Shakespeare it was melodrama; for Dostoyevsky, the *feuilleton*; for Hegel, philosophy; for Aristophanes, the "gag."

Advice to Myself. May your every word, at very least, be reticent.

The music of Vivaldi is pure conversation.

A great artist is a lifelong diligent apprentice to himself.

The secret to André Gide is that he made puberty last until he was eighty.

If the Ecclesiast had sincerely been as pessimistic as he says, he wouldn't have written his book.

The Death of the Goethian. They say that Thomas Mann's last words were: "Where are my glasses?" In practical terms, the phrase is just as valid as "Light, more light!" (August 1955)

Joan Miró has a touch of the Holy Spirit. (Or: If the Holy Spirit painted, he would paint like Joan Miró.)

There is a class of writer who might be defined as "gentlemen who have never read Plato." Pío Baroja, for example.

Liszt: A sacred orator.

Half of every novel is superfluous.

The work of Franz Kafka leans toward what used to be called the "philosophical story." Strange as it may seem, this is in line with Swift and Voltaire. And the *Quixote*. And certain recent fables, like *Brave New World*. On the understanding, though, that behind Kafka's "philosophical tales" lies not so much philosophy as desolation.

Does the poet truly say what I understand in reading him? It doesn't matter. He makes me *understand* something. And if it is not what he says, it is what I was just about to say to myself.

Eugeni d'Ors? Are you kidding? That old French right wing intellectual!

On literary style. Simplicity is not always compatible with exactitude.

The great superiority of Mozart resides in his *still* being an Italian musician.

"...*Aboli bibelot d'inanité sonore*..." Isn't all abstract painting, at heart, pure visual inanity?

As a general rule, modern Catalan literature is a literature created by satisfied, sedentary, undeceived husbands—and priests. This is why it most definitely feels bland and, above all, repetitive.

The truth is that jazz, and all its imitations and derivatives, has ended up making everyone a little mulatto.

With all due respect, Marcel Proust seems to me to be the perfect literary equivalent of a chiclet. You know, chewing gum.

Adjectives are always subjective.

Shakespeare. The best passage from *Romeo and Juliet* is Tchaikovsky's overture.

And in the end who knows whether it wasn't Romeo's destiny to be cuckolded!

To describe is to inventory: a subordinate, secondary activity, meant for notaries or bad novelists.

Beware of those who speak ill of Descartes! They will end up making a case for Pascal, and you know what that means.

One qualifier for the painting of Hieronymous Bosch: dissolute.

Some literary styles are incompatible with the typewriter.

Given a more or less suggestive vocabulary, philosophy is *almost* a question of syntax, just as poetry is *almost* a question of prosody.

Ultimately—the way things are going—valuing culture for its degree of utility may perhaps be the only way to save it.

We write with our enemies in mind. Either to convince them or to corrupt them.

Rameau's harpsichord has a toothache.

Say what modern-day painters and critics may, the essential thing about portraits is the resemblance: the physical resemblance. But it is also true that this—this resemblance—is only interesting to the model and their closest family.

I greatly admire the work of Salvador Espriu, among other, more serious, reasons because he has introduced a bit of Semitism into the heart of a literary corpus with as many Hellenic pretensions as 20th century Catalan literature.

Someone observed that no statue has ever been erected to a critic. Which is perhaps one more reason for critics to be reaffirmed in their vocation.

Joyce. *Ulysses* could only have been written by a devout pervert, the depraved graduate of a parochial school.

Mauriac says that the purpose of novelistic literature is "knowledge of man". Of the man who writes it, at very least, I would say.

It is surprising how much nonsense we can spout—and what is worse, with a clear conscience—by using a quote from an illustrious author as a shield.

A Question of Musical Aesthetics. To determine whether a flat is as expressive of pain as Schopenhauer asserted, or if, in fact, what it expresses might be less pain and more hunger or the categorical imperative.

I think the poetry our times call for ought to be informed by rage or sarcasm. Or just by rage, because, in the long run, sarcasm is just rage attenuated by cunning.

Montaigne. Referring to his own writings, he said: "*Mes songes que voici…*" Wouldn't it have been better to say "*Mensonges que voici…*"? And if this applies to Montaigne, it applies to everyone. To write is to dissemble.

Preferences. Picasso or reality. Miró or joy. Klee or silence. Chagall or truth.

If you are capable of reading Huxley in massive doses, you will end up imagining him as a fearsome, incessant, prodigal, miraculous, useless thinking machine.

The bad thing about Wagner is that, inevitably, he seems to be lying.

Mr. Navarro Costabella used to say—or they say he said—that the greatest novelist ever known was Tolstoyevski. But this depends how you look at it, because he could also be the worst.

We invented archaeology and we must suffer the consequences. That is, to be the topic of discussion ourselves when our time comes.

Bad literature may be written with the finest sentiments, or with the most perverse sentiments. In general, bad literature is always being written—above all on the basis of sentiment.

It's just incredible how much nonsense Baudelaire wrote in verse. Who could ever have imagined it!

Believe me, this is a recommendation from the bottom of my heart. Read Bertrand Russell. He is not a philosopher, he is a disinfectant.

This is the truth: Fortuny is a great painter, and Salvador Dalí is not.

As you well know, in poetry there are theories that rest on inspiration, while others give precedence to calculation. There are good *inspired* poets, and good *calculating* poets. Still, if you look closely, inspiration is just a calculation, so quick and so mysteriously automatic, that it hardly seems to be a calculation.

There is only one serious way to read, and it is to reread.

What we mean by the word "musician", that is, thoroughbred musicians, is Mozart, and Chopin, and Ravel, and Corelli, and Tchaikovsky and Telemann and Vivaldi, and even Mendelssohn. But not Bach, or Beethoven, or Wagner, or Debussy, or Stravinsky.

Oddly, Plato was a great reader of Aristophanes. Works by the lewd writer of comedies were found under the pillow of the philosopher's death bed. It is a shame that Kant, Hegel, and Heidegger did not share his literary predilection.

The Risks of Exegesis. A critic can end up believing that the work he is commenting on has been written *exclusively* for him to fulfill his function as a commentator.

It is indeed likely that Picasso has begun to decline, as some critics assert. Why should this surprise us, though? This is a right the old painter has more than earned.
(1959)

Walt Whitman had the virtue of not seeing the sordidness of sordid things. This is why he was able to write songs to himself, to the multitudes, and to his country.

No. Our dear *bourgeois gentilhomme* had no right to affect surprise. He did not speak in prose. No one speaks in prose without knowing it—that is, without knowing how. Indeed, only lecturers speak in prose.

I have never been able to hear the final choruses of the Ninth Symphony as if they were music, but only as what they really are, that is, a hymn. Still, I am not entirely sure I have ever found them to be a hymn to joy, but rather to something else altogether. I'm not sure what, but something more noble.

Neo-scholasticism. Maritain—Maritain, et al.—reminds me of that advice from the Gospels not to put a patch of new fabric on an old garment, because you will waste the patch, the garment, and, in the end, your time.

Books are no *substitute* for life, but life is also no substitute for books.

All verse is already written. Let us speak of poetry, then.

Look at Nefertitis' beautiful visage, or Michelangelo's David, or Doña Cayetana's improbable body. Where, oh death, is thy victory?

Goethe is odious—like a mountain, or a downpour.

With Dostoyevsky it is hard to tell where his Christianity ends and the consequences of his epilepsy begin (or vice versa).

From certain vantage points, *Das Kapital* is also escapist literature, in a manner of speaking. It is just a question of *what* one is trying to escape from.

A happy man feels no need to express himself.

Poems that sing of luck in love have been written *afterwards*, in a moment of tedium or desperation—and as a way to alleviate them.

When Stendhal predicted that his oeuvre would be understood around 1890—give or take a year—he could easily have added that it would cease to be understood around 1990.

As a critic of the modern world and its alleged aberrations, Papini—that is, the Papini of *Gog* and of *Il libbro nero*—reminds one of a little pedigreed lap dog: naughty, cute, noisy, given to barking but not biting. And, above all, ultimately a nuisance with its pointless, tiresome games.

In truth, if you give it enough thought, it turns out that the important poets have always confined themselves to writing about the moon.

In Rodin's nudes you can tell that the clothes the figures have just taken off are the rough industrial garments of the 19th century. On the sculptures' surfaces there is something akin to the outline of a cheap undershirt.

Poe—he himself said it—was artificial by nature. While most of us—poor devils!—try to be, or to appear, natural by dint of artifice.

Renan. An incredulous and erudite nun. But, a nun, nevertheless.
(I ask myself how I could have wasted so much as an hour reading him.)

Metaphors—good metaphors—are nothing but unforeseen definitions, saying the same thing but in a surprising way. It is a way of disguising their triviality, and that's why poets make such copious use of them.

D'Annunzio was, personally, the falsest character of his own literary oeuvre. Which is saying a lot!

It may conceivably be over the top to claim that the unsung krewes of New Orleans are the direct descendants of Frescobaldi or Pergolese, but you must grant me, at very least, that Cole Porter and Irving Berlin are the sons of Puccini.

A writer's first obligation is to be readable.

Having carried out a fairly perfect statistical calculation on the total mass of Catalan literature produced since the Renaixença, the results I find vis-à-vis the question of theme are as follows:

a) 60 per cent is a more or less academic gloss of those Verdaguer lines that go:

May all be for Thee
baby Jesus so sweet;
may all be thy love
Jesus, little dove.

b) 30 per cent deals with the Empordà;

and

c) the remaining 10 per cent deals with the same topics as are custo-mary in any civilized literature.

Contrary to Goethe. There is nothing *sublime* which, expressed in a certain way, does not appear humorous.

Sade, Maldoror and company have never really managed to interest me. Systematic monstrosity seems too easy, and too dreary.

There are painters who are greatest when they are painting most badly. Example: the Goya of the black paintings. But this phenomenon only occurs when the painter is already great to begin with.

I feel great envy for Carles Riba if in real life he is as happy as he claims to be in his poetry. (1951)

Little reading distances one from life. Abundant reading draws one near it.

"Life is short and art proves to be long…" The translation is from Ausiàs March. Hence, it is not recommended to follow the counsel "slowly but surely". So, either do it quickly, or forget about it.

Some pianos are enervating. Debussy's, for example.

The two greatest poets of the Spanish language in the 20th century are Latin American. The first, naturally, is Pablo Neruda. The second, that gentleman whose name I can't quite recall—an Italian surname, I think—who wrote the lyrics to Carlos Gardel's tangos.

In Other Words. The History of Philosophy is that chapter of the History of Literature where the great unreadable books are squirreled away.

It would appear that there are many kinds of romanticism. Henry Miller, for example, is a romantic. To be precise, a sort of romantic Aretino—a sad, anarchistic Aretino. Not all romantics are romantics of the heart. Some are romantics of the groin.

"*Was bleibet aber, stiften es die Dichter*". Which means—they say—"Everything that lasts has been founded by poets." The assertion of a poet, naturally.

Rule of Thumb. "Like any writer known as an essayist, Zapata occasionally contradicts himself…" (M. Menéndez Pelayo, *Orígenes de la novela*, cap. IX).

I'm not sure why, but Mendelssohn's violin concerto makes me think of Shelley.

Paul Valéry. Yes, yes, whatever you all say. But you can't eat diamonds.

After reading Lukács, one comes away with the impression that it is very difficult to produce literature without playing into the hands of capitalism. And the worst thing is that it's true.

For a writer, bile can be a fine stylistic ingredient.

FOR THE ONE, FOR THE MANY

Quis custodiet ipsos custodes? That is the question! *Et tout le reste est littérature.*

"Command" equals "contempt". (And, what's more, "He who pays, commands.")

Only if you see history as a permanent expiation will it cease to appear absurd and criminal. But then, of course, the very fact of the expiation will also appear absurd and criminal.

If multitudes are brutish, violent, indecorous, and blind, it is because they are made up of individuals who are, more or less, like each and every one of us.

"*No surgen las ideas de los puños*". Ideas don't rise from fists. Clearly. But our ideas are different after a punch. Particularly if we are the ones being punched.

France. In reality, the *Marseillaise* is simply Mr. Chauvin's daily aphrodisiac.

Still, there is an appreciable improvement in the shift from seeing work as punishment to seeing it as merchandise.

You will often have heard the principle which holds that "the end doesn't justify the means." Take note, though, of who proffers it. You will see that, in most cases, it comes from a gentleman sitting in an armchair, who doesn't care to remember how he came to be sitting there, and who wishes even less to be made to get up.

When Farouk of Egypt was dethroned, a traveling salesman wisely commented: "These days it is a mistake to be king."

War, hunger, oppression... The daily crimes of our society are as monstrous as they are persistent. The worst crime of all, though, is having become so inured to them that we have become complicit out of indifference.

"The property owner, that prehistoric animal..." Indeed!

The great lovers—those deserving of the honor of poetry or of annals (Romeo and Juliet, Paolo and Francesca, Hero and Leander, the Aga Khan and his wives, etc.)—are usually well-to-do. Love is an exercise of the rich—or of the idle, if nothing more.

As they say in Valencia, if you have a tongue, you're bound for Rome. But we might also say if you have a tongue, you came from Rome.

Cogito ergo sumus. And that's that.

There are two kinds of Christians—two ways to profess any ideology: those who tend to remember that "whoever is not with me is against me" (Math., XII, 30), and those who believe that "whoever is not against us is with us" (Luke, IX, 50).

The most tempting thing about revolutions is that one never knows where they might lead.

The sins—or vices—condemned by traditional ethics are neither arbitrary nor gratuitous. Look closely and you will see how they all—every one—turn out to be socially unprofitable.

Justice is the most corrosive idea man has invented. With it, he dares to challenge God, upend society, and murder his neighbor. But it must be recognized that, without it, he would in fact be nothing but a pitiful, abject victim.

The history of Italy is a gorgeous opera. What tenors! What stage mechanics! What scenery! And those choruses!

In every historical moment, all "lost causes" are lost for the same—profound—reason. This gives them common cause. The day their supporters catch on, their causes begin to be winnable, if not already won.

More than a seer, a prophet is a provocateur.

Prophets are full of indignation. This is why they only prophesy catastrophes.

"*Hierusalem, Hierusalem…*" Imagine people did not stone their prophets. What would happen then?

On the other hand, history only remembers the prophets who were right.

On the Destiny of Western Civilization, and so on.—I don't know why. Surely because we have reached a high degree of saturation. Of saturation with…, all of it. It need not be specified. But the fact is that I am seized by a violent desire to write a poem that would begin like this:

Oh, Lord, send in the barbarians!
Don't let us deserve them more!

Mutatis mutandis. Fear the man who reads only one newspaper (Saint Augustine).

Europe's malady is that there are still millions of Jacobins in need of civilizing.

A slave rarely rebels. A man in the depths of misery, of *absolute* misery, tends toward suicide or resignation. An uprising, even a social uprising, only emerges when the oppressed begin not to be oppressed. That is to say, when the oppressor has let up a bit, out of negligence or good will.

The most repulsive aspect of dominating peoples may be their imposing on the dominated people the spectacle of their insoluble mediocrity. The case of Rome is not unique.

Conducting Literature. Since we "cannot keep a bird from singing", it is advisable to teach it harmony.

Needless to say, that gentleman who cries out and protests, aghast, against demagoguery does not belong to the *demos*.

Often cinema has been described as the "art of the masses." It would be better to call it "art against the masses." All the tyrannies of our time—*nec nominetur*—have made use of the stultifying power of the movies to dull the social and human sensibility of the spectator. To be precise, capitalist cinema is the opium of the people. Propaganda films are another kind of opium, with identical soporific effects, but no pleasant dreams.

Violence engenders violence. But—let us not forget—tolerance also engenders violence, and despair engenders violence, and—above all—truth engenders violence.

Antigone's error was to forget that, at the last minute, the gods take the side of the powers-that-be.

Totalitarian State? Isn't that a tautology?

In certain countries, religious persecutions have a touch of the crime of passion about them: "*La maté porque era mía*" … "I killed her because she was mine…"

Technics. "Oh! More than one organ of death was born of a cool calculation…" Indeed, Mr. Rilke!

It is a fine thing to discredit heroism, because a hero is always both a dangerous creature and a demoralizing example. But it can be just as dangerous to let go of all reserves of heroism. So long as the enemy doesn't relinquish their heroes, we would be well-advised to cultivate our own. If only to be able to counter theirs, when push comes to shove.

I don't know why we give the words *plebe* and *plebeian* a negative charge. I'm a plebeian and even so I don't consider myself at all worthy of disdain.

On the Historical Origins of Strikes. One, in Greece. Aristophanes records it in *Lysistrata*. It was a sex strike.

"*Salus ex judaeis est*". Maybe they were thinking of Marx.

Judging by the comments of authorized observers, the English tend to be a caricature of the English.

I find it strange that many who praise or admire Napoleon tend, in contrast, to disparage or vilify Ramon Cabrera. In the end, as humans—not as pillars of ideology or military strategists, of course—I see only one important difference between the two of them: Napoleon killed (or ordered to be killed) many more people.

The day that the merits of rancor are accounted for it will become clear that they are not insignificant. Without rancor we would not have the Revolution, or Nationalisms, or most of the *Divina Commedia*.

Laws are written by those who are in a position to respect them—and only *because* they are in this position.

What's more, all laws have the same purpose: to protect trade. And that explains everything.

"*Don Quijote, Don Juan, Don Me…*"
Yes, milady! "*Your faithful and attentive servant, who kisses your hands, Pepe.*"

It really was necessary for the nuclear bomb to be invented. For too long humanity had lost one of the most ancient habits of Christian civilization, the belief in an immediate end to the world. And now we have recovered it.

"*Littérature engagée.*" It is my impression that everything that is not literature of resentment is just literature of consent.

Illustrious experts in dogma assert that man's knees are meant only, or fundamentally, for kneeling. Whence are derived, as could only be expected, harsh political and religious theories.

A politician is opportunistic, or he is not a politician.

In war, in any kind of struggle, each party finds a way to do what he supposes the rival party would do in the same situation. The suppositions in question, of course, are usually eminently reprehensible. We can derive peace of mind, however, in thinking—to say it in the words of the people—"to do as others do is no sin." Except that this, in truth, is the same as a simple and unacknowledged "do as I do."

Everyone is liberal *up to a point*, and I don't know a single anarchist who is not an anarchist *only* up to a point.

I am not entirely sure whether Europeans *are* the grandparents of the Americans or whether in fact we *will be* their grandchildren.

The great joy of the bourgeois is that he is bourgeois without knowing it.

Antonio Machado said of Castile, "*Wrapped in its rags, it looks down on what it knows not.*"
Joan Maragall said of the Catalans, "*They tend to laugh at what they don't understand.*"
Given a choice, I don't know which is worse. Except for the rags, of course.

The true end of a war is not the ensuing peace, but another war.

In property as in love—which is yet another form of property—what is essential is not so much to enjoy the thing or beloved one has, as to deny others such enjoyment. (One could also say: "In love as in property—which is yet another form of love—what is essential..., etc.).

Anyone willing to die for an ideal is just as willing, at heart, to kill for said ideal. A doctrine that starts out with martyrs ends up with an inquisition.

No one demands freedom except to exhibit one form or another of impiety.

There have always been tyrannies, and almost certainly there always will be. The most bearable among them are the ones not exercised in the name of elevated principles.

The only genuinely positive politics is the so foolishly maligned "bell tower politics," the politics that deals with concrete problems and petty passions. The other kind of politics—higher-order politics—is just novelizing: rhetoric and adventure, half and half. Often catastrophic, or, in the best of cases, pointless.

It is important to foster conscientious objection, not only against war but also—or above all—against certain forms of peace.

It is good to feel tribal ties. It is a way of having dead, gods, and progeny without having to produce them yourself.

If you look at History, you might come to believe that the Germans have launched wars—so many wars!—simply for the pleasure of being defeated.

"It is just as difficult for the rich to acquire wisdom as for the wise to acquire wealth." This is what Epictetus said, who was poor—a slave—and, naturally, wise. In this world, sometimes you have to make do with cold comfort.

When things go badly for the settlers of the Iberian Peninsula, they accuse one another of being individualistic, and they think that explains everything.

Leisure is essentially pernicious. The day that machines, automated or more productive, grant man almost continuous free time—it could happen—the ravages will be plain to see. For example, a growing predilection for alcohol, philosophy, and suicide.

The myth of the *bon sauvage* was not entirely stupid. The civilized always feel a bit wicked when faced with their conscience.

History teaches us that the only important defect of reigns of terror—that of the French Revolution and so many more—is that, to judge by the events that succeed them, they were always *insufficient*: too short and not intense enough.

When the Russians learned to add, the charm of the "Slavic soul" soon faded.

The Idea of the Homeland. The old Latin adage, serious and utilitarian, says: "*Ubi bene, ibi patria.*" Huysmans, devout and spiritual, says: "*Ma patrie c'est où je prie bien.*" In the long run, the two attitudes are equivalent.

Society won't be fooled. It knows that madness is only a biological alibi for certain types of nonconformity. More than a place of healing, a sanatorium acts as a prison.

It is logical that all Marxists be more Marxist than Marx.

"*Summum ius, summa iniuria.*" But we need not reach the extreme of "summum." All *ius* is in essence *iniuria*, in certain social conditions—ours, for example.

One thing people of all races, including Jews, tend to agree on: hatred of Jews. (Perhaps I exaggerate, but not all that much.)

They say—I am no expert—that, given equal conditions, the same causes will produce the same effects. Most likely. But not in history, where the effects just get worse and worse.

We must be wary of those who preach the idea of sacrifice. They need someone to be sacrificed *for them*.

Comic dialogue.
First character: "*Dieu et mon droit!*"
Second character: "What did he say?"
Third character: "God and the right of this gentleman."
Second character: "Ah!"

A weak person—no matter what kind of weakness is in question—is always a delinquent. Lawyers will attest to it.

To be persecuted is a victory in itself.

According to Scripture, each people has its wise man and its mad-man (or—or *and*—its fool). And also its just man and its evil man. Without them, of course, *the others* perhaps couldn't feel like a people—like *one* people.

We believe that when a crime is *necessary* for one reason or another, it ceases ipso facto to be a crime. And this is clearly a sinister conviction. A necessary crime is still a crime and must be treated as such.

Seize the first opportunity that presents itself to establish yourself as an accuser before someone else does. You will have won half the battle.

It is dangerous to take literally the advice to let the dead bury the dead. The "departed" will not take up the task. And, unburied the former and the latter, they start to smell... or end up convincing us they're still alive, and this complicates things considerably.

Naturally, those who govern lie out of fear.

Enthusiasm? It's no help in building a house, writing a book, or tilling a field. It isn't even a help in playing soccer. The only thing you can do with the help of enthusiasm is sing—and poorly, at that.

For the poor, money is a mystery. This is why they remain poor.

You could conceivably constitute a political party anywhere whose sole program would be opposition to the absurdity of the other parties.

It seems strange that man has taken so long to invent museums, large, comfortable armchairs, the tango, sociology, vacations—and so many other things that have nothing to do with the progress of science. Perhaps we are not such intelligent animals as we would like to think we are.

Thàlassa! Thàlassa!... Yes, but from the shore.

Patria is—also—war, *id est*, commerce, just as much as medals and cemeteries.

You can only be cultural when it's time for coffee to be served. After a meal, I mean. Can a man half dying of hunger take an interest in the problem of the *analogia entis*, or the prosodic particularities of Dante, or quantum theory, or even the concept of surplus value?

It is incomprehensible that the French of 1793 could have made a revolution singing the *Carmagnole* and *Ça ira*. They sound more like country tavern Easter tunes. Or, perhaps it is not "*le ton qui fait la chanson*"?

"Success is a justification," said Napoleon. Failure, too. Or neither one nor the other justifies anything. Or—even better—nothing can be justified.

All flags are equally tricky. Trust more in the flag-bearers than in the colors.

Force is still a means of persuasion. With one proviso, though. It is the slowest and most fragile one we know. In general, few people are disposed to being persuaded by any means. Not even by force.

Don't get your hopes up. Power changes hands, but it rarely vacillates.

Naturally, pessimists come from the right. In point of fact, what can someone who has nothing to lose fear? (But sometimes I wonder if everyone is not from the right—in one way or another, at least?)

GENERAL ABSOLUTION AND
PLENARY INDULGENCE

And, when all is said and done, what then? We are all going to die. Nothing we can do about it.

So forget about it.

Good day, dear reader, future cadaver, future nullity. *Sit tibi terra levis!*

DISHONEST
PROPOSITIONS

EARLY WARNING

"Propositions," indeed, but only in the sense of an "enunciation of a judgement," to quote Fabra.

And isn't any "proposition" also a "purpose" and a "proposal"?

I have always thought that "honesty" was a concept stipulated by others.

OBSERVED BY CHANCE

There are useful deceits. Geometry, for example.

No matter what is at their literal core, interjections always have the air of a spell.

Life—alas!—is so fragmentary!

Where there is a great deal of light, everything looks a bit obscene.

Tedium justifies anything. A bored man can do any deed without batting an eye.

We say "*idée fixe.*" But then it is no longer an idea.

To be passionate one must enjoy very good health.

The hardest part of the body to persuade is the sex. Or the easiest, depending how you look at it.

True crimes are clandestine.

Sometimes imprudence yields good results.

Love is not a question of love, but of skill.

People who appear to be making concessions—a young woman, a politician, a salesman—are actually only waiting to demand their own.

The only consolation is ignorance.

To be honest, dogs are not so much faithful as they are worshipful.

Appearances are not deceiving. They are appearances.

The most noxious parasites we can bear are our detractors.

Everything depends on words.

Man invented man, and that is why he is man, or appears to be. (Variation, or rectification: Man has created man in his own image and likeness. It is what it is.)

The only truly ambitious person is one who has no hope of success.

Nothing creates a stronger bond than a shared delusion.

Elegance is expensive—even that form of it known as "natural elegance."

From a certain point of view, no matter where we go, we're always late to arrive.

Nowadays, sighing has fallen into disuse.

The most painful thing to lose is what we have not yet possessed.

Women live. Men, in general, think they live.

Often we call a hostile will "an error." It is a hasty attribution.

Some people are stupid out of sheer laziness.

Skeptics are right to be skeptical, but they are almost never as skeptical as they ought to be.

Living is bad for your health.

Good habits can also corrupt us.

It is precisely because we are carnivores that we need veterinarians.

Sometimes a set of stubborn habits can appear to be a credo, an ideal, or a theory. There are people whose lives depend on obstinacy.

Roses are immoral, don't you agree?

Our hands are always empty.

Indifference is eminently diurnal.

Irritable temperaments tend toward austerity, fanaticism and—beware!—betrayal.

We are sincere to the extent it behooves us to be, and not a bit more.

Life can come to seem so improbable that we haven't even fully imagined it.

It's a shame, but 2 plus 2 does not make 4, except on paper, and maybe not even there. Perhaps saying on paper that 2 plus 2 make four is just a pleonasm.

Everything takes practice. Even pain.

Humanism. Man would never have "invented" the sea.

…The serious drama at the core of kitsch…

A fiasco doesn't happen by accident.

A woman is a man who is so absolutely alienated that she isn't even a woman.

To sleep is also to wait. Or to hope.

Doesn't the word *parvenu* seem a bit archaic nowadays?

No one can live life without creating a victim. Or without becoming a victim to himself.

When someone rises in judgement of his brother, he has already decided to condemn him.

There are people who yawn while making love.

Happiness … Happiness, let us state it clearly, consists of any form of abuse.

In certain situations, silence can be the most loathsome form of slander.

To die at night is much too easy.

Fatigue leads to incredulity.

You have to be a bit cynical to choose to protect plants and animals.

People say: "To do as others do is no sin." Or to put it another way: "The more, the merrier."

Some men deserve to be cheated on. And if they aren't, it's the wife's fault.

Put-downs are usually frivolous. To craft a good insult, a proper, honest-to-god insult, you need a cool head and steady nerves.

In the long run, a good reputation isn't good for much.

There are hardly any misanthropes anymore. Not a good sign.

And what about chastity? Isn't it a form of avarice?

In the long run, we are what others allow us to be and, often, what others want us to be.

There are no innocent joys.

They say rage is blind. A lucid rage. Now that would be ideal.

We live by dint of patience. But we are not aware that it is, precisely, a question of patience.

The husband is always a comic figure.

A "swindle" consists of getting someone to believe precisely what they want to believe.

All our acts are incomplete.

Luxury is a sort of disguise.

The face we make when we're sleeping is beyond our control. It shouldn't be held against us.

No one admits it explicitly, but the bidet is the totem of our times.

We tend to be too indulgent with our own weaknesses and this, come to think of it, is the weakness most deserving of indulgence.

When we're in the dark, we turn on a lamp. And then we call that "light".

Vinegar is still wine.

A frustrated sectarian bears quite some resemblance to a skeptic. Careful, though!

There is praise that constitutes a veritable aggression.

Family is also a question of talent.

Idea from the Driver of a Stalled Car. When God sleeps, machines break down.

Adulthood is only reached when the son begins to feel compassion for the father. No matter what the law says.

At the hour of death, everyone owes a rooster to one Aesculapius or another.

NOTIONS FOR YOUNG GENTLEMEN

When we say "I have the right to," we are already cheating.

Sadly, there is no point in scratching if we don't have an itch.

Ultimately, love is just a venereal disease like any other.

Happy people have no memory.

In principle, teeth are meant for biting. Revealing them in a smile goes against nature.

The way the world is going, the day will come when being young will be grounds for admiration.

And isn't sleepiness a vice?

If you think about it, the act of lying obliges us to be aware of the truth.

Your brother has no confidence in you. Nor does your wife, or your father. They must be onto something.

All excesses have the virtue of alerting us that they are precisely that: *excessive*.

It is deliberate, ergo, it is unforgiveable.

Strength is never innocent. Not even an athlete's strength.

To *speak* of a passion is the equivalent of reducing it by half.

Misfortunes can also be ridiculous.

Try as we may, we can never be as impassive as we would like.

We are sentimental out of frivolity.

Sometimes what appears to be an adversity is just a simple misunderstanding.

Between lovers, jealousy can only be wielded in legitimate self-defense.

If you make a promise, you are already consenting.

Money is only a conjecture.

The unforeseen is an obstacle.

Forgetful people always have a clear conscience.

In certain circumstances, to slander is to speak the truth or, at very least, to invent it.

Blessed are the timid, for they will abstain.

Solitude is exhausting. Company is exhausting. There is no solution.

Luck befalls the lucky.

At the heart of all voluptuosity there is almost always a sophism.

Those who understand do not admire.

Past joys are generally bitter memories. Dante *dixit*. But they are because we want them to be.

An error is, among other things, a faux pas.

We are often called upon to fulfill our duties disloyally.

They call it "an offense to virtue," but it is just life.

And who doesn't feel like a deserter?

Yes, indeed, the world is a mess... At very least, let's say so from time to time.

The ideas are clear. The feelings, confused.

A person who looks at a flower and thinks of fleetingness is perverse.

Men seem more human when we have a touch of degradation in our lives.

The mirror accuses you. Look closely and you will see how.

If you are earning money, you exist.

You have to have a lot of will power not to become a murderer.

Love allows us to be idiots with impunity.

To pretend... Is it worth the trouble?

Rage is an opinion, too.

Any defect you have will always be a lesser evil.

Danger is attractive because it's a change in routine.

Sometimes abnegation is a form of irony.

The only thing that saves us from feeling envy is self-respect.

There is no satiety for the lecherous. And who is without lechery?

We haven't learned it. We have been inculcated with it!

It is irritating to be the object of compassion. And the time always comes when love is a barely disguised form of compassion.

Meditation at the Fountain. To drink without thirst. That would be more human.

We believe what it is in our interest to believe. Nobody wants to be a sucker in this valley of tears.

There is only one peaceable way to live. Asleep.

Not nudity, but clothing, is indecent. But we've become accustomed to it and, on top of that, the climate calls for it.

"Bad advice" is usually pointless. The only people who heed it are those who don't need it.

We say that something "disgusts" us, but the truth is that it frightens us.

When a stupid man speaks, he pollutes the air around him.

They are the people.

In the end, death is not just dying. It is dying and being forgotten. Short or long term, forgotten.

It seems that fasting excites the imagination. But maybe satiety would excite it even more.

Beyond a certain critical point, belief in God is incredibly audacious. Let's at least give credit where credit is due.

They have coffee, they drink cognac… Why, then, are they against pornography?

Irony requires complicity.

It's all well and good that you declined those "honors." But it was suspicious to have deserved them in the first place.

Seeing things just as they are predisposes certain people to be bores.

People say "guests and fish stink on the third day." To be honest, on the third day everything stinks: guests, fish, pure poetry, quantum physics, Buddhist thought, and you, yourself.

Morality is more a question of ideas than of behavior.

There are very malevolent ways of doing good.

Depending how it is presented, lack of appetite can even come to seem like an abstention or a sacrifice.

And what if we are all just apocryphal characters?

PERSONAL EXPERIENCE

It's not that I like to say "I." It's just that I have no right to speak with any other personal pronoun.

I am an optimist: I close my eyes.

My contradictions are my only hope.

En enfer je recevrai des coups de bec de toutes les perdrix que j'ai tuées (J. Renard). And so will I. But that's fine with me.

I don't care if someone cheats on me. What really pisses me off is knowing they're cheating on me.

Anyone who puts up with me, loves me. There is no other explanation.

I am going to die, I am going to die, I am going to die... What a shame (for me, above all)!

And to die must be to stop writing.

It's when I'm alone that I can think of others.

What most interests me about my (let's say "my") ideas are the objections I myself can pose to them.

Every oversight is an amputation, without my realizing it.

There are times when I think the clock is unfair.

I am—I think I am—a Jew. Aren't you?

After a certain age, I consider myself happy if I don't have a toothache.

Oh, if I could only choose my reasons for being indignant!

I try to be aware of what I don't know.

As for me, I'm happy just to be a *little bit* "right" *from time to time*. To aspire to more seems depraved.

I am afraid, and I cry out. I am afraid, and I am silent. Either way: I am afraid.

I live—to put it some way—*quia absurdum.*

Since I don't dare say what I think, I do my best to say what I ought to think.

Who truly knows all his aversions?

We are born, and people are happy. We die, and people cry. I don't really get it…

I am my superstition. The superstition of myself.

People hate me, and that is of no importance. But they oblige me to hate them, and that *is* important.

I imagine how others see me, and I feel a little sorry for myself. But, then, I think about them, and I realize it's not all that bad.

The weak are *doomed* to be disloyal, dishonest, envious, and sneaky. So don't hold it against us!

Him (to me): I share your opinions.
Me: I share them, too, of course. But only so far…

My adversary is my collaborator. *Malgré lui*, of course.

You accuse me of being sarcastic. And why shouldn't I be? I can barely put up with myself!

Everything I now think and write about, has been thought and written about by many, but very very many, people before me. If this were not so, what would be the point?

I am perpetually convalescing from my prejudices.

I abhor intransigence because it is catching.

The worst thing about being old is that everyone, at first blush, wants to show you respect.

Do people argue with you? Well, then, you have some probability of being right.

When push comes to shove, we always end up falling in love with the shape of a nose.

We are bought and sold. I do not belong to myself.

Sad to say, we rarely have the memories we would like.

There are pieces of nature that seem unfinished.

We all have moments in which we would like to be perfect idiots.

It is a shame not to have had an implacable critic at our disposal when we most needed them.

Past the frontier of forty, you start to perceive your despairs as comical.

Only the rich have immortal souls.

Socrates, Mayakovsky, Pavese? It is the suicides of the illiterate that chill me to the bone.

I spy on myself and, this way, every so often, I figure out what I am doing.

I think of you. Is it possible you're just an optical illusion?

Love letters are always sad.

We usually say "he talks to himself" with scorn. But everyone talks to himself when he doesn't have an interlocutor at hand.

I am probably mistaken. Even so, I must run this risk.

To be me is unfair.

As In the Days of Julien Sorel. "People are afraid of losing their jobs" and "the only pleasures left are reading and agriculture" (*Le Rouge et le Noir*, I, cap. VII).

When I can't find an opponent, I try to imagine one.

Don't obsess about it. You are anthropomorphic by chance.

Behind every spoken or written word, how much unnecessary ferment!

In the morning all birds sing the same song, just as at night all cows are black.

It is very hard to achieve certainty, and even so it is always temporary.

"*Piangerò la sorte mia...*" But in verse or to opera music.

My posterity will be on paper.

We may not like our own faces, but we don't mind this or that portrait of ourselves.

A poet once told me: "An untimely toothache can frustrate a master-piece."

In villages you can still find the occasional lingering or instinctive Nietzschean. I am acquainted with one who asserted: "Piety is a vice of the gods..."
But he had a propensity for sarcasm.

"Guilt"! What a word!

They say, "You are what you do." And they are right. "I am what I produce." All that surplus value stuff *y compris*...

Fire. The speed!

The idea of "reciprocity" is astutely selfish. And it explains the existence of "good Samaritans."

Every day we discover we are neophytes in something.

What do I know of you? What do I know of myself?

I don't know why, but in practical terms, stud animals do not seem indecent, and families with a lot of children enjoy considerable advantages.

If at least there were a devil we could make a pact with!

Everyone is subaltern to someone.

I have confidence in letters. Any written word, either *per se* or *a contrario sensu*, will always end up being revolutionary. It is simply a question of knowing how to read.

Freedom and migraine are incompatible.

No matter how you look at it, logic is a comforting device.

Try it yourself: The allegro in Vivaldi's Concerto n. 1, opus 12, for violin and orchestra can be danced as a fox trot.

We live furtively. Why?

For a skeptic the need to hurry is an inadmissible concept.

Sometimes, the alternatives are: Trip or back up.

HUMANITIES

Literature consists of talking about literature.

To think is to deform. As in painting or poetry, but in a different way.

Pedagogy. To know is to know how to repeat.

When I look at a painting, I see it as I wish.

It's a good thing Hegel is so hard to read. If not, nowadays everyone would be a Hegelian.

The cello has the voice of a sacristan—at very least, of a cantor.

People don't blaspheme as much as they used to. If I were monotheistic, I'd start worrying.

Poets' hatreds are feminine.

An honest intellectual begins by writing a sentence. The rest of his oeuvre will be nothing more than a series of rectifications of what he wrote the first day.

Exactitude is also an art.

In reality, only philosophers respect philosophy. And not all of them, either.

To some extent, every painting is a self-portrait.

On Originality. Together we can all think it all.

Reading Kafka is masturbating without pleasure.

"And, who is my neighbor? Jesus Christ declares it thus: any person of whom there can be benefit." In truth, I don't know if Jesus Christ "declared" it thus, but Saint Vincent Ferrer certainly did (Sermons, II, 91). What's more, the definition is lovely.

When a painter paints, the world grows.

Artists are not required to justify their work. They are always right on principle.

Perfection tends to drift toward mediocrity. Nevertheless, it is necessary to seek perfection. The secret probably lies in stopping mid-course.

The greatest human creation is the equilateral triangle.

"*Le Philosophe sans le savoir.*" In a certain sense the only one deserving of forgiveness.

Poetry is only good for making more poetry.

Why didn't Archimedes, Pythagoras, or Euclides invent the bicycle? Was it laziness, indifference?

T. S. Eliot was Queen Victoria's grandson.

The erudite never get bored, and this is the only explanation for the verdant overgrowth of the historical sciences.

A statue is a ghost. Sculptors and spiritualists will tell you I'm wrong, but it's true.

Hamlet... A graft of Buffalo Bill and Hamlet—now that would be an interesting person.

To correct and augment: This is culture.

No one imitates in good faith.

Topic for a Doctoral Thesis. To identify the precise moment in which Robinson Crusoe begins *once again* to feel the need for a philosophy.

Painting *au naturel*? With his brushes in hand, a painter need only look at the canvas before him.

Senyor Puigblanch, of Mataró, had occasion to write, in Spanish: "As these sins are born of an excessive love for the propagation of the species…" (*Opúsculos*, II, additions).

All ideas end up suffering from rheumatism.

Like the earth and the heavens, *ennarrant gloriam Dei*, callipygian young ladies proclaim the glory of God. A senile opinion, if you wish. A good apologia, nevertheless. How is it theologians haven't capitalized on it?

A good book is always a provocation.

Someone invented art to make up for the deficiencies of truth.

It was when we decided that killing a tiger, a chicken, or a flea is not the same as killing a man that we became men. But this doesn't happen every day.

Dodecaphonic music is too thorny.

They say gold has a standard conventional value. Balzac, too.

The idea of abjection must be secularized, just as some countries have secularized cemeteries.

It's easy to read, but how hard was it to write?

Perhaps, and in contrast with the classic opinion, art is short, and life, if not long, at least relatively long.

Health, good health, preserves you from philosophy. Personal hygiene, for example, is "anti-metaphysical"—at least in a functional sense.

Apostasy is out of fashion. Nowadays it is only practiced by princes and princesses of marriageable age, and indeed purely for reasons of State.

To write is to remember or, in any case, to invent memories.

Only what is evident is reasonable. Reason, to a large extent, depends on "vision."

History of Painting. "*Non saturatur oculus visu.*" (*Ecc.*, 1:8.)

The sexes of the rich are more pathetic than those of the poor. As certified by Petrarch, Shakespeare, Corneille, Dumas fils, Proust, Lawrence…

It is still too soon to preach hedonism.

In the western world, no grammar would be conceivable without Aristotle's *Logica* as a basis.

In art, the fairest form of realism is the caricature.

Good thing Goya didn't know how to paint! Otherwise, I'd feel sorry for the family of Charles IV!

What must the Neanderthals have thought about "human dignity"?

There also exist intellectual astigmatisms, and it must be recognized that they have made no little contribution to the prosperity of culture.

Stendhal. It is enough for the "details" to be "exact" ("*voici des détails exacts*"). Nothing else matters.

Truth is always a mystification of the truth.

(Possible) definition of philosophy: The art of grabbing a cow by the balls.

For more than a millennium, western culture has been elaborated by priests and the alumni of priests. We can't shake them off from one day to the next.

Impressionism was painting to "pass the time."

The danger of "mastering the technique" is for art simply to become "technique."

"*Ce qui est noir n'est peut-être qu'obscur...*" Look sharp! Colors and words do not have neat borders.

Lot's wife didn't look back out of curiosity, but out of malice.

I have read excellent critiques *contra* the venerable institution that is the Syllogism. But they were also written using syllogisms.

The shim-shim of the musicians of the 17th and 18th centuries has one advantage. It is soothing. Like symmetry.

Pearls from the Dictionary: Philosopher. "*Filosop (phil-, filosof)..., 2, Patient urinal*" (*Diccionari Aguiló*, vol. *IV*, p. 57).

Mathematicians are a sort of fraudulent poets who, in fact, attempt the only possible poetry.

In art, memory is a mistake.

Might El Greco's figures have been syphilitic?

Any premeditated sound can be considered music.

Materialism. Dialectical or not: for the moment, that is secondary. Insofar as materialism is philosophy, it doesn't even resemble philosophy. What more could we ask?

Only archaeologists know what time is.

THE ART OF GIVING ADVICE

Never turn your ignorance into an argument.

To assert yourself, you need a rival. Don't destroy him, preserve him! Subsidize him, if necessary.

Be discreet. Practically absent.

If you don't retaliate, let it be out of disdain.

May your intentions always be good. They may end up serving as an alibi.

Shy away from excessive gratitude. It is usually sincere and, hence, cause for annoyance.

Compare, and you will begin to understand.

Do not ask for clemency. If it is conceded, it will be in bad faith.

You have a body. Use it, enjoy it!

You think *this*. You think you think *this*—whatever it may be… Well, then. Try to rethink it. Rethink it. You will see how, in effect, you thought *something else*.

We must be scrupulous. Above all, when the time comes to choose our scruples.

Love, but a little less.

Spare no effort in kicking down open doors. If you don't, they will be shut again.

The more friends you have, the more you can lose.

Don't write poetry about death. It's pointless. Write a will. It's much more practical.

Tell the truth. This is your revenge.

If you listen when people speak to you, you will end up speaking yourself. This is a warning.

Amphitryon invites you to lunch. Say with me: Long live Amphitryon!

Enmity is not complete unless it is reciprocal. When you find a prospective enemy, don't let them slip away.

Be courteous: Believe what your wife tells you.

Do not stop protesting. Something will always remain of it.

No, pay no mind to those who speak to you of the grandeur—moral grandeur, of course—of pain, and run to get some aspirin.

We must trust in chance. Not much, but a little.

It's not enough to have a mattress in the house. We must use it to be born on, to sleep on, to fornicate on, and to die on.

With a little bit of luck, you will end up believing that you are you.

If you have children, teach them to be free. Even if it is at your own expense. In truth, it will have to be at your own expense...

Not everyone has the prerogative of doubting. Do your best to doubt anyway.

Recant, when you are asked. But try not to be asked.

Don't have more convictions than are decidedly indispensable.

When you have insomnia, try writing poems. I am sure many a great poet started out this way.

Don't be insolent. They'll think you're being sincere!

Don't ask questions, because they will answer, and you never know what.

It is delightful to be asked for something. It is even more delightful to say no.

Warning! Be sure to administer your ingratitude wisely!

If you ever cry—in reality or metaphorically—let it be premeditated.

Knowing who your friends are. This is the secret.

When you refuse to speak of this or that, your refusal speaks for you.

What about you? Aren't you a "bad influence"?

Define yourself, if you will. But don't lose sight of the fact that to do so is to show your dirty laundry...

Grease your own palm, before someone else does.

It's a bad sign if your opinions are not the consequence of your passions. Even worse if your passions are the consequence of your opinions.

Don't abstain, while you still can.

Let that fellow persuade you, if you like. On condition, however, that you be equally disposed to letting yourself be persuaded by the next fellow.

At whose expense? Ask yourself this, from time to time.

Monotony also has its charms and, what's more, it is respectable.

As a literary genre, the "aphorism" is in decadence. Do not attempt to cultivate it.

Persevere and... you will end up bored to tears.

First you must figure out what cannot be remedied. Then you must figure out how to resign yourself it.

If you don't have money, let it be.

Hide. If they find you, let it be by chance.

It is in our personal papers, which no one is meant to read, where we must be particularly careful not to make spelling mistakes.

If anything, camouflage your stupidity with ill humor.

Let others make assertions. Meanwhile, prepare your rebuttal.

In the age of cybernetics, what matters is to know how to switch off a machine.

Only the humble never feel humiliated. Do not be humble.

Choose whatever is to your advantage, but don't try to justify it.

Don't accept defeat until you find you will benefit from it.

Someone looks you in the eye, and it is disconcerting. But they feel seen in the same way and are just as disconcerted.

It makes sense to be on your guard.

If you want to be held in esteem by others, pretend to be like them, but better or worse.

A "happening," you say? That would be a sight to see, staged at the factory gate.

Plan ahead. Make sure your shroud is in your size.

You are your neurosis. But, if you can, see a psychiatrist.

I urge you to learn how to ride horseback. In the coming classless society you will not have this opportunity. True, you don't have it now, either. Still, I urge you to do it. It's so decorative.

It's important to have a seat. Wherever. Somewhere.

You should read Henry Miller because, to be perfectly honest, you would hate Rabelais. And, when push comes to shove, with either of them, you will discover the inexhaustible, instructive, epic of the loins.

What are you up to now? This, *in itself*, is a senile passion.

If you persist, let it be in bad faith.

They treat you like a thing. And the thing is, you are a thing, quantifiable and with a market value. It is your obligation to know it.

Five bodily senses! We demand more!

"Tomorrow is another day" and "The day will never come." Let's start over, then.

Since you seek recompense, be smart. You are not entitled, and you will have to fake it.

A well-played violin, a barbiturate, a dose of alcohol…

Don't be your own matchmaker. That's no fun.

"Nothing is too petty/and no hour is too dour…" wrote Salvat-Papasseit, dead of tuberculosis at the age of thirty. Cold comfort.

Like in children's games: "Close your eyes and stick out your hand…"

THEY CALL IT "SOCIETY"

In the end, idleness can also be considered an ideology.

One of the first episodes of the class struggle was the invention of the lock.

No one can demand serenity of his victim.

When fear is not innocent, it is no longer fear, but cowardice.

I attain a bit of liberty. Then I ask myself, at whose expense?

You eat, you chew. In practical terms, when your mouth is full, you are gagged.

One's *per capita* sexual income! This, too, should be statistically tabulated.

"*Saintes baïonettes de France…*" (Michelet). Every war wants to be a holy war.

Those in power want those in their charge to be docile. Every philosophy of history should start with this obvious fact.

They shout to see if they can shut us up.

"Wealth is the slave of a wise man, the master of a fool." Seneca said it. Who, naturally, was a rich man.

Racism. Blacks are not the same as Whites because they are Black.

The only revolutions worth fearing are the premature ones, because they end badly.

"*Puix parla en català...*" The old saying goes "Since he speaks Catalan, God give him glory." But an equally correct decasyllable would be "Since he speaks Catalan, let's hear what he says". And the content is more reasonable.

The myth doesn't say that Prometheus dies. We should bear this in mind.

"*Les capacités de la bourgeoisie s'en vont...*" As M. Guizot shows, the bourgeoisie just doesn't know how to be left wing anymore.

Some women are fearless. They even dare to have grandchildren.

The aspiration to abolish private property runs up against a difficult obstacle: the prehensility of the hand.

Qui paga, mana? He who pays is in control? History and daily experience demonstrate, at the very least, that he who is in control, gets paid. To be in control is to get paid—among other things.

If nothing more, Frederick the Great had over Hitler or De Gaulle the virtue of knowing how to compose music.

The defeated soon go out of fashion.

It may be that work dignifies man. I don't know. But there is no question that it exhausts him.

In the so-called "consumer" society it neither rains, nor snows, nor does the sun come out.

Someone once said that the kepi deforms the head. But not just the kepi. Also the salakot, the skullcap, the top hat, the beret, the bowler, and—needless to say!—the *barretina*.

Before there were judges, there were surveyors. The latter are the premise for the former.

On the eve of a war, it often, or almost always, feels like a party.

Conservatives enjoy obedience, and that's why they're conservative.

They fight sperm as if they were Koch's bacillus.

There are people in government for whom governing is simply an exercise in revenge.

Who was it who declared that "you can do anything with bayonets except sit on them"? No, no. Some butts are capable of sitting anywhere.

There are times when blood stains are decorative. Read Plutarch.

"*La liberté consiste à ne dépendre que des lois...*" Oh, Candide, oh innocence. As if *they* didn't make the laws!

A person begins to be rich at the point when they fear becoming poorer than they are now.

Lenin, or Marx, or both of them, said that until now all revolutions have ended up reinforcing the machinery of the state. Reactions to revolutions, too. The machinery of the state is always reinforced, with any excuse.

As Eugeni d'Ors pointed out, the *sardana* is "republican" and "federal." And maybe this is why it is in decline.

"All Power Comes from God." But where do the powerful come from?

People are enemies of equality, of egalitarianism, among other, more solid reasons, for fear of seeing themselves as "too equal."

Dictatorship is intoxicating.

When has the censure of egoism not been done in the name of another egoism? (In parallel: When has the censure of nationalism not been done…, etc., etc.?)

It is quite easy to be right wing. You need only forget that one can be right wing without realizing it.

Any idea, or ideology, can be used to justify a crime, and history is full of such cases. Naturally, the bad thing is not the crime, but the justification.

Genesis, iii, 19. But since sweat evaporates…

They are soldiers, torturers, con men by trade… Can't they find a better way to earn a living?

Democracy is unstable. Which is why everyone fears it.

"*Du pouvoir absolu vous ignorez l'ivresse*," proclaimed a character in Racine. Or, as someone else seems to have said closer to home: *¡Da tanto gusto mandar!* "It is such fun to be in command!"

Our vocabulary is blighted with classism. We speak of "noble gases" and we say that a dog "without a master" is "abandoned," instead of "free."

The only advantage to being an underling is not being an overlord.

Wars should be fought by the old. It would be biologically less onerous.

Moreover, wars are always declared by old men.

Multitudes rise up or they obey, but they do not reason. This is the problem. It's a waiting game...

All power is abuse of power. This is in the very nature of things.

What Republic would not give in to the temptation of being defended by a Bonaparte?

Freedom is a habit, and it is not at all easy to come by.
It only comes with practice!

I have observed that right wing people are even more right wing when it rains.

Ethnography and Folklore. Silence struck fear into man. And so he devised the drum. Then, with the drum, he organized wars and dances.

At this point in time, a revolution can only be sacrilegious.

Your political adversary will accuse you of not doing what you ought to do, and of doing it, if you did it. This is part of the game.

No hymns, no flags, no *vivas*.

They say that tyrannies always end badly. Maybe. But, as the tyrants say, *it was fun while it lasted!*

Regicide is out of fashion. That Kennedy thing was an anachronism.

We must never tire of repeating it: All freedoms are acts of solidarity.

Observed from without, we will find that in every "system", heresies are more fearsome than orthodoxy.

The way things are going, to be Catalan nowadays is nothing but a simple hypothesis.

"Non-intervention in the Internal Affairs of Another Country." Jaume Bofill i Mates (*L'altra concòrdia*, p. 50) defined it thus: "Sovereign powers giving each other reciprocal *carte blanche* freely to oppress their subjects."

Who can say why, but the poor tend to vote for right-wing candidates. And the rich, too, of course.

Painting has the disadvantage, vis-à-vis literature, of not being able to be immoral, or to be immoral only when it is no longer authentically painting.

Power secretes a patrimonial conception of power. The owner is the one giving the orders.

We breathe as we did in Paleolithic times. In this regard, we haven't come very far.

Is a living dog worth more than a dead lion? It depends on the why and the what for!

How to maintain discipline. Philippe Pétain said it and did it (June 12, 1917): "*Une première impression de terreur est indispensable, et c'est aux premiers exemples qu'est due l'amélioration constatée...*" (Gilbert Guilleminault, *La France de la Madelon*, p. 159).

When all is said and done, one flock of geese or another saves the Capitol.

PROVISIONALLY CLOSING
THE PARENTHESIS

Debatable assertions and negations, I admit it. Maybe it's precisely because they're debatable that they'll be useful. Because they stimulate discussion.

EPILOGUE

Biographical note

Joan Fuster is a unicorn.

He lived through all the convulsions of a very convulsive 20th century Spain. Born in 1922 during the dictatorship of Primo de Rivera, he was nine years old when the Spanish Republic was declared (1931), thirteen when General Francisco Franco's troops rose up against the Republic (1936), and seventeen when the Spanish Civil War ended (1939). Soon after, he matriculated in law at the University of Valencia, graduating in 1947, traversed all the years of dictatorship, and when Franco died in his bed (1975), was an important figure during the transition to democracy and the subsequent period of cultural and political optimism.

Fuster's family were conservative Catholics, Carlists (adherents to Don Carlos, a 19th century Bourbon pretender to the throne) from a farming background, but Fuster's father was a woodworker who made a good living replacing the church statuary destroyed by anticlerical forces before and during the Civil War, also teaching drawing at a local high school.

Fuster said of his childhood, "Like any other postwar child from the provinces, I grew up in utter ignorance intellectually, and under the doctrinaire intoxication of the Dictatorship." As he himself tells it in the author's prologue included here, there were few books in his house. He said elsewhere of his father, though, that he was a "rather odd" Carlist, "a Carlist of popular extraction, which is to say, a sort of right-wing anarchist," who fortunately, gave him leave to read anything he wanted in others' libraries. And did he ever. When Fuster graduated from law school he had accumulated a library of a thousand books; when he died, he left a library of 25,000 volumes to his hometown, Sueca.

On graduating, Fuster practiced law for a couple of years as he published his first poetry collections in Catalan. He soon abandoned his law practice to devote himself entirely to writing, mostly in Spanish, in newspapers and journals in Valencia and Barcelona. Apart from a few journals under the umbrella of the Catholic church (e.g., *Serra d'Or*, published by the Montserrat Abbey from 1959 on) and some reviews published by Catalan exiles, in Mexico and elsewhere, Catalan was largely prohibited in periodical literature. Fuster published his first article in Catalan in *El Pont Blau* (*The Blue Bridge*) in Mexico in 1944.

With no career in law, Fuster was impelled to be incredibly prolific, practically ubiquitous, in the Valencian and Barcelona press. He once remarked that to write an article, "…you start by putting a sheet of paper in the typewriter. When you have written for more than an hour and a half, you have begun to lose money." He did translations, travel guides, prefaces and prologues, satirical pieces for humor journals, and somehow found time as well to write scholarly articles on both contemporary peers and the great Valencian Renaissance authors.

In 1962 Fuster published *Nosaltres, els valencians* (*We, the Valencians*) a book that would establish his fame and, in some sense, his notoriety. Concerned from early on to understand and define the particularities of Valencian culture—as he put it, "impassioned almost to the point of obsession by the life and destiny of my people"— in *Nosaltres, els valencians*, he proposed a view of Valencia as part of the *Països Catalans*, the Catalan Countries, a cultural continuity with the Principate of Catalonia and the Balearic Islands. This commonality was based to a great extent on the shared language and culture brought to both Valencia and the Balearic Islands during the 13th century conquest of the Arabic-speaking territories by Jaume the Conqueror, King of Aragon and Count of Barcelona. Fuster's pan-Catalan perspective—rather astonishing at the height of full-bore Francoism— raised hackles on the right and caused some dissension among others who saw it as putting Valencia in a position subservient to Catalonia. Fuster lamented that someone else, a historian or a sociologist, or a "centaur" combining the two, in his words, had not taken on the task of defining the Valencian psyche. However, in the absence of such a mythical creature, he took up the gauntlet. The aftereffects were still felt in 1981, when anti-Catalanist ultra-right zealots set two bombs off at his house in Sueca. There were no victims of the blast, but his library suffered extensive damage.

At the start of this biographical note, I said Fuster was a unicorn. Perhaps I should have said he was a miracle. In an interview with Montserrat Roig, he once stated, "I sprang from myself." To put it another way, he was erudite, but self-taught. He was a hermit, who rarely left his home in Sueca, twenty-three miles from Valencia— perhaps venturing out to buy whiskey, books, and records—who nevertheless lived squarely in the contemporary cosmopolitan world. He was a humanist, in pan-secular dialogue with Heraclitus, Aristophanes, Plato, Nietzsche, Marx, Dante (and more Dante), Goethe, Rilke. In a word, the entire cast of Western civilization, including Cervantes and Goya, as well as such great Catalan and Valencian figures as Vicent Ferrer, Joan Maragall, Carles Riba, and Joan Miró. Indeed, he coupled heady philosophical commentary with a great interest in art and music, and a strong dose of unabashed sensuality. Here is a small sample: "Try it yourself: The allegro in Vivaldi's Concerto n. 1, opus 12, for violin and orchestra, can be danced as a fox trot." (I picture him swaying in his library.) Or, "Five bodily senses! We demand more!"

Best of all, there is his sense of humor. Fuster's wit reveals that the best aphorisms are based in stripping language of its artifice and revealing its contradictions. (Early in the book, for example, Fuster declares that "In essence, euphemisms are already lies.") Many of the revelations in this book actually work like one-liners, setting up a premise based on one sense of a word, and undermining it in the follow-up. The cumulative effect is a quintessentially Mediterranean kind of irony, leavened by playfulness. At times Fuster is a little bit closer to Groucho Marx than to Cioran, and that is one of the joys of this book.

Notes on the translation

A new and fascinating collection of essays on translation, *Violent Phenomena*, edited by Kavita Bhanot and Jeremy Tiang (Tilted Axis Press, 2022), makes the point in the prologue that "translation is a fundamentally political act." Their concern, and that of all the collected essayists, revolves mainly around translation into English. That is, both the history and current problematics of cultural appropriation, bowdlerization, fetishization, surveillance, and other pitfalls of bringing cultures seen as more "marginal" into the tent of the overweening centrality of English, and of a "mythical English reader," as posed by Anton Hur. It is this rather obtuse creature whom publishers are always brandishing when it is they who want to say no: an English reader won't buy a book with the translator's name on the cover, an English reader will question this syntax, etc., etc.

These fundamental questions of power also play out in a translation into English from Catalan, from any of the variants of Catalan—a minoritized language spread out over several regions of Spain—Catalonia, Valencia, the Balearic Islands and parts of Aragon—and spilling over into France, Andorra, and Italy. A complicated geography for a language spoken by 9-10 million people, but one in which a common problem is shared: diglossia, or the presence of two languages, or two registers of a language, in a hierarchical relationship. The pairing of an official language such as Spanish or French, spoken by many tens or hundreds of millions more people, with a language like Catalan, delimited by geography (it is only official within the confines of the Catalan-speaking territories, but not co-official in the rest of the country), and law (recently, for example, the courts of Spain decreed that 25% of class time in Catalan schools must be devoted to Spanish), and by other intangibles such as relative prestige, resistance to use, presence of other languages—always Spanish, then English, and now Russian, Rumanian, Chinese, etc.,—is fraught with difficulty. Even in their own country, there are situations—hospitals, courts, sometimes even cafès and restaurants—in which Catalans are not able to speak Catalan.

Joan Fuster was very much aware of these issues, as they were even more egregious in the years when he was writing about them, mainly the 1960s and 70s. He addressed them in many articles from varying perspectives, going from a defense of translation as cosmopolitanism, to a concern for the loss of authenticity—the intangible "genius of the language," which he admitted no one could define—through a flattening of the idiolect by the uniformity of translation, of importing language that will rub away the distinctive traits of the local language. In a different article, though, he took a stab at defining this "genius": "In the end, a linguistic unity is always the correlation of another, sub-jacent, unity, composed of a living society or of persisting inertias." Inertias composed of the substrates of cultural habits and codes that were further undermined by translations, "in the case in which a third language interferes in the mechanism," that is, when the works are translated into Spanish. (Though, probably to dodge the censors, he never actually mentions the word).

Still, I would like to counter the anxiety expressed in the collection of essays I opened with, and posit a useful and constructive role for translation, in this case into English, though it holds for any language: into Basque, into Hindi, into any other language but the one with which it forms an uneasy tandem. Translating Catalan into English, in this case translating Joan Fuster into English, releases him and his text from the hierarchical assumptions that inhere to the relationship with Spanish. A text translated from Catalan into English exists on an equal footing with a text translated from any other language or written originally in English. Its success or failure will depend on its quality, and the vicissitudes of the market.

There is a naïveté in this. Bhanot and Tiang would rightly object that many books published originally in English have large budgets, famous authors, fancy covers with no distracting names of translators to discourage their purchase. And big advances for the author that need not be shared with a translator. But, still, many do not. And the liberation of being read through English, undermining the assumptions of local minoritization and, at least in literary terms, existing on an equal plane with all the other languages translated and with English itself—well, this is a very healthy exercise, if nothing more.

Translation, indeed, always signals a border crossing, with the inherent dangers of such a passage, and a bending of rules and usages in both the source and the target language. There is a continuous process of measurement in a translator's labor: is this too foreign, am I being too colloquial, is this a false cognate, did the rhyme obscure the reason?

In *Final Judgements* some accommodations have been made, and some have not. When I first started translating these aphorisms, I faced a steep learning curve. In light of the copious references to Greek and Latin authors, and the liberal quotes from Italian and French, I wondered if I, with no Latin and a less than robust background in philosophy, were the right person to translate the book. I also wondered if we—my publisher and editor, Douglas Suttle, and I—would have to include a bulky and distracting glossary of terms to appease Anton Hur's mythical English reader. Ultimately, I concluded both that I *was* the right person, and that we shouldn't include a bulky lexicographic apparatus.

It was Fuster himself who gave me leave, with this aphorism: "I try to be aware of what I don't know." And this is the true second sight of a translator, to sense when the sense of a word is not the most obvious one, to discern and research and refine until the author is living in our head, and we can interrogate them, and practically channel them. And we have to trust that a diligent and loving reader will make the same effort and go to the dictionary, or the encyclopedia, or, more likely, google the same phrases I did.

Some of the challenges were philosophical; some were temporal. Much water has gone under the bridge since these aphorisms were written, largely in the 1960s. There are attitudes and assumptions that are, in a word, cringey to our current sensibilities. This was the first sentence that tripped us up: "The truth is that jazz, and all its imitations and derivatives, has ended up making everyone a little mulatto." On the one hand, this aphorism is written in a spirit of admiration;

on the other, the word "mulatto" is offensive to a broad range of people, though there are those who defend its use. I tried substitutes: "biracial," "black and brown," "persons of color." But each of these solutions simply gave rise to another series of problems or objections as 21st century anachronisms. The problem is not with the word; the problem is with the problem, and the descriptors we use for race and color in a racist society are constantly evolving, and always insufficient.

In the end, we have left it as is. First, we can't change history: Fuster used a word that has almost exactly the same charge of political incorrectness in Catalan as in English, now and, perhaps, in 1967. And second, there are scattered instances in the book of correspondingly incorrect statements about other often othered groups: Jews and women. The aphorisms about Jews are similarly admiring; the ones about women are not. Frankly, the latter are so outré that sometimes I don't even understand them. But we decided it was unfair to Fuster to censor him, and unfair to the reader and to posterity to try to hide this aspect of his work.

I can only hope that these flaws, important, but hopefully not fatal, have not been an impediment to your enjoyment of the book.

Mary Ann Newman